Veg Recipes
Vegetarian Cookbook for Beginners

40 Easy Vegetarian Meal Prep Recipes to Make at Home

By Brendan Fawn

Table of Contents

Vegetarian burger with cucumber, avocado and champignon
Vegetarian farm burger with potatoes, tomatoes, onions and corn
Delicious zucchini, walnuts, corn and sweet bell peppers rolls
Raw Gazpacho with grapes, strawberries and dried tomatoes
Spaghetti from a zucchini with mango and blueberry sauce

Cherry smoothie with almond milk
Rice pudding with coconut milk
Chocolate mousse with mango and almonds
Light pumpkin, coconut and orange mousse
Kiwi and yogurt with walnuts and honey
Blueberry cocktail with yogurt and honey
Yogurt with banana
Kiwi and banana mousse
Strawberry mousse
Conclusion

Introduction

The popularity of vegetarian and vegan lifestyle is growing every day around the world. People are choosing this lifestyle due to the health, ethical, moral, cultural, religious and other reasons. In coming years, we will most likely observe a growing demand for vegetarian lifestyle and ideology.

I want to be the tiny part of this worldwide movement, ideology, and lifestyle, therefore I have decided to publish this book with vegetarian and vegan recipes which are simple to cook, but contain plenty of vitamins.

This book is written not only for vegetarians and vegans, but also for people who want choose a healthier lifestyle, or just want to try new tastes and experiences.

You don't need to be a professional 28 Michelin Star chef to use recipes from this book and to cook for yourself, your family or friends! I would like to encourage you to test those recipes and to experiment, not always strictly following the recipes given, but adding your own flavors and tastes!

Truly Yours,

Brendan Fawn

Chapter I: Soups

I have decided to start this book with something light and essential for our stomach. Light vegetable soups are the best option for everyday use to hold our stomach in perfect condition for the long run.

Spring zucchini soup with avocado, celery, basil and lemon juice

This light spring vegetable soup with zucchini and avocado will help regain your strengths. It is perfect for children, as well as for starting a supper after a long day!
If you like, you can add more herbs and aroma spices or even sprinkle with chili. Lemon juice will add some liveliness. Also if you want the soup to become more tasty and nutritious, serve it with delicious paste-like coconut cream and whole wheat bread!

Completion: 20 min
Prep time: 10 min
Cooking time: 10 min
Servings: 2

Ingredients:
30 oz of sliced zucchini
1 avocado

1 onion
2 cups of basil leaves
1 large sliced leek
3 chopped celery stalks
4 chopped cloves of garlic
5 cups of water or vegetable broth
2 tablespoons olive oil
1 teaspoon dried oregano
1 lemon
salt and pepper
fresh basil leaves

How to Cook:
1. Heat the oil in a large kitchen saucepan. Add the onion, celery, salt and fry vegetables about 5 minutes until soft.
2. Add the garlic and fry for another 40 seconds.
3. Add the zucchini, fry for a minute, and then add half the basil and water.
4. Cook, stirring occasionally until the zucchini is tender for about 15 minutes.
5. Add diced avocado and cook for 5 min.
6. Add the remaining basil and whip up the soup with a blender.
7. Squeeze lemon juice and add it to the soup.
8. Add salt and pepper. Serve with olive oil, diced avocado, and basil!

Nutritional Information:
Calories: 320
Total fat: 1 oz
Total carbohydrates: 2 oz
Proteins: 1 oz

Spring sunny carrot soup with mashed potatoes and onions

There's more than one reason why many people love creamy soups. Each creamy soup is made of fresh vegetables which create a stunning combination of flavors, spices, and smells. This cheerful, sunny, orange color spicy carrot soup is rich in beta-carotene and is perfect for early spring cold days, thanks to spices.

Completion: 25 min
Prep time: 10 min
Cooking time: 15 min
Servings: 2

<u>Ingredients:</u>

35 oz of carrots
2 medium onions
2-3 cloves of garlic
1 large tomato
2 potatoes
2 tablespoons olive
0.5 inches piece of ginger
½ teaspoon coriander
½ chili
1 teaspoon curry powder
3-4 cups of water or vegetable broth
½ cup coconut milk
salt, black pepper
herbs and fresh greens up to taste

How to Cook:

1. Peel the carrots, potatoes and garlic.
2. Peel the onions and fry in olive oil in a large saucepan over medium heat until clear.
3. Add spices (coriander, chili and curry powder), diced carrots, shredded ginger, and garlic. Fry for 5-7 minutes.
4. Cut the tomato and add it to the carrots.
5. Cut the potatoes into cubes, add to a pan and fill with water or broth. If you want to get a thick soup, add less water. First bring the soup to a boil and reduce the heat to medium. Cook until carrots with potatoes are soft.
6. Whip up the soup with a blender.
7. Pour coconut milk into it, season with salt, pepper and stir.
8. Serve with garnish and coconut milk.

Nutritional Information:
Calories: 350
Total fat: 1 oz
Total carbohydrates: 1 oz
Protein: 0.9 oz

Fiery tomatoes soup with milk

This unusual recipe of warming fiery tomatoes soup with milk will be a remarkable addition to your daily menu. I'm sure you'll definitely add it to your favorite recipes!

Completion: 40 min
Prep time: 15 min
Cooking time: 25 min
Servings: 4

Ingredients:

3.5 lbs of red tomatoes
7 tablespoons olive or sunflower oil
1 teaspoon ground coriander
4 tablespoons chopped coriander
1½ tablespoon brown sugar
1½ teaspoon salt

¼ teaspoon ground pepper
¼ teaspoon ground red pepper
2 tablespoons butter
2 tablespoons white flour
1.5 cup of milk
1 tablespoon lemon juice

How to Cook:

1. Whip up tomatoes with a blender.
2. Fry ground coriander in oil in a saucepan for few seconds.
3. Add smashed tomatoes and cook in a large saucepan over medium heat for 20-25 minutes.
4. Add chopped coriander, brown sugar, salt, ground pepper and red pepper.
5. Add butter into another saucepan and cook with flour until light dark color.
6. Pour milk and stir over until thickened.
7. Mix the sauce with tomatoes and add lemon juice.

Nutritional Information:

Calories: 500
Total fat: 2.5 oz
Total carbohydrates: 1.9
Protein: 1.5

Asian coconut milk soup with pumpkin

Veg Asian coconut milk soup with pumpkin has a very tender and pleasant soft taste. Your relatives and family will always ask for more! To prepare this warming and aromatic soup with coconut milk, you will need a spicy pumpkin and very little time.

Completion: 30 min
Prep time: 10 min
Cooking time: 20 min
Servings: 4

Ingredients:
30 oz of pumpkin
1 large onion
15 oz of coconut milk
2 cups of water
sunflower oil
4 tablespoons of roasted pumpkin seeds
a piece of ginger, not bigger than a hazelnut
pepper, salt
fresh greens

How to Cook:

1. Peel the pumpkin, cut into cubes and put into a pan. Pour the water and boil for 20 minutes.
2. Cut ginger into small pieces and send into a pan. Fans of hot chili could add a small piece of it.
3. Cut the onions, fry it in oil, and then add into a pan with pumpkin.
4. Roast pumpkin seeds in the same frying pan. Add into a pan together with salt and pepper.
5. Add coconut milk, cook for 5 minutes.
6. Add chopped greens.

Nutritional Information:

Calories: 220
Total fat: 1 oz
Total carbohydrates: 1 oz
Protein: 0.8 oz

Soup with tomato and eggplant

Number of vegetables in this soup could be changed easily, depending on what vegetables you have in your kitchen. There is only one vegetable that couldn't be changed - the eggplant.
Completion: 30 min
Prep time: 10 min
Cooking time: 20 min
Servings: 2

Ingredients:
1 tomato
1 eggplant
1 onion
1 bell pepper
2 potatoes
1 chopped garlic clove
2 tablespoons white flour
olive oil
salt
ground pepper
red pepper

How to Cook:
1. Peel the onion, potatoes, bell pepper and cut them into cubes.
2. Add vegetables to a pan and fill with water or vegetable broth. Boil for 10 minutes.
3. Cut tomato into cubes and cook with vegetables for 5 minutes.
4. Cut the eggplant into rings, and fry in oil. Add some flour.
5. Cut eggplant rings into cubes and add to the soup.
6. Add some salt, ground pepper and red pepper.

<u>Nutritional Information:</u>
Calories: 489
Total fat: 3 oz
Total carbohydrates: 1 oz
Protein: 0.9 oz

Onion soup with potatoes and spinach

It is tasty and fast to cook. You can use frozen spinach which can be kept safely in a fridge, but you can use fresh spinach as well.

Completion: 40 min
Prep time: 10 min
Cooking time: 30 min
Servings: 4

Ingredients:
4 onions
3 potatoes
2 chopped garlic cloves
2 carrots
4 oz frozen spinach

sunflower oil
lime juice
salt
ground black pepper
red pepper
Herbes de Provence
fresh chopped parsley

How to Cook:

1. Peel and cut potatoes into cubes, boil them for 15 min.
2. Peel the onions, cut them and fry in oil until golden brown.
3. Peel and then cut carrots into rings.
4. Add carrots, onions, garlic, frozen spinach to a pan and boil for 15 min.
5. Add lime juice.
6. Add salt, ground pepper, red pepper and Herbes de Provence.
7. Add fresh chopped parsley.

Nutritional Information:

Calories: 275
Total fat: 1.5 oz
Total carbohydrates: 1.5 oz
Protein: 1 oz

Light soup with cauliflower, broccoli and tomatoes

Light soup with cauliflower, broccoli and tomatoes is very delicious and fast to cook. It is rich in vitamins due to various vegetables. Your family will love it.

Completion: 35 min
Prep time: 5 min
Cooking time: 30 min
Servings: 4

Ingredients:

8 oz cauliflower
8 oz broccoli
4 potatoes
3 tomatoes
2 onions

2 chopped garlic cloves
1 carrot
4 spoons of soy sauce
sunflower oil
salt
ground black pepper
red pepper
Herbes de Provence
fresh chopped parsley

How to Cook:

1. Peel and cut potatoes into cubes, boil them for 15 min.
2. Peel the onions, cut them and fry in oil until golden brown.
3. Cut cauliflower, broccoli, tomatoes, garlic and carrot into pieces.
4. Add vegetables to a pan and boil for 15 min.
5. Add salt, ground pepper, red pepper and Herbes de Provence.
6. Add soy sauce and fresh chopped parsley.

Nutritional Information:

Calories: 315
Total fat: 3.5 oz
Total carbohydrates: 2 oz
Protein: 1 oz

Chapter II: Salads

Vitamins and microelements are vital for our health which is why we should include fresh vegetable salads into our daily eating routine.

Delicious fresh salad with beets, prunes and walnuts

If you like different tastes in one dish including sweet, sharp, spicy and crispy, then beet salad with prunes, walnuts and garlic will be the best option for you! Thanks to prunes and beets, it makes your stomach feel magnificent. Beet cleans the body and the blood. Moreover, it is also very tasty!

Completion: 20 min
Prep time: 10 min
Serving: 2

Ingredients:
1 large baked or cooked beet
1 sour apple
half cup of prunes
half cup of walnuts
1 tablespoon olive oil
1 teaspoon white wine vinegar
1 chopped garlic clove
salt
black ground pepper
red ground pepper
ground coriander
chopped fresh parsley

How to Prepare:
1. Peel the beet and apple, cut them into cubes.
2. Put the beet and apple into a bowl.
3. Cut prune into cubes and mix together with walnuts.
4. If using greens, chop it and add to a bowl.
5. Add salt, pepper, garlic, ground coriander and mix well.
6. Mix olive oil and vinegar in a small bowl. Add to a bowl with vegetables. Mix well and serve!

Nutritional Information:
Calories: 220
Total fat: 1 oz
Total carbohydrates: 1 oz
Protein: 0.9 oz

Colorful light summer salad with a fresh vegetable mix

Summer is the colorful time when everything comes to life. Colorful light summer salad is easy to make and packed with summer colors and vegetables. Your family will adore it!

Completion: 15 min
Prep time: 10 min
Serving: 2
Ingredients:
2 big carrots
1 onion
1 big and fresh cucumber
5-8 radishes
1 pomegranate
2 tablespoons olive oil

small bunch of chives
2 oz arugula
2 oz Tatsoi plant
2 oz Mizuna mustard greens
2 oz mustard plant
2 oz fresh young beet leaves
salt
black ground pepper
ground coriander
chopped fresh parsley

How to Prepare:

1. Peel the carrots, onion and cucumber.
2. Grate carrots, onions, cucumber, radishes.
3. Chop chives and mix with other vegetables.
4. Add arugula, Tatsoi, Mizuna, mustard plant, young beet leaves, salt, pepper, coriander and parsley.
5. Add pomegranate seeds.
6. Pour olive oil and serve!

Nutritional Information:

Calories: 180
Total fat: 1 oz
Total carbohydrates: 2 oz
Protein: 1 oz

Salad with arugula and orange

Would you like to try something new? Then salad with arugula and orange is for you! This mix of different tastes and colors will be a wonderful new experience.

Completion: 10 min
Prep time: 5 min
Serving: 2

Ingredients:

1 ripe orange
4 oz arugula
4 oz spinach
4 oz lettuce
2 tablespoons of canned corn
2 tablespoons olive oil
1 red onion
1 teaspoon brown sugar
lime juice
sea salt
freshly ground black pepper

How to Prepare:

1. Peel the orange.
2. Cut orange into segments.
3. Chop arugula, spinach, red onion and lettuce and mix with orange.
4. Add corns.
5. Add sugar, salt, pepper.
6. Pour olive oil and lime juice over the salad.

Nutritional Information:

Calories: 201

Total fat: 0.5 oz
Total carbohydrates: 0.4 oz
Protein: 0.3 oz

Salad with arugula and mango

If you would you like something light, healthy and easy, then salad with arugula and mango is for you!

Completion: 10 min
Prep time: 5 min
Serving: 2

Ingredients:
1 mango
5 oz arugula
4 oz lettuce
2 teaspoons brown sugar
3 tablespoons lemon juice
sea salt
ground black pepper

red pepper

How to Prepare:
1. Peel the mango.
2. Cut mango into cubes.
3. Chop arugula, lettuce and mix with mango.
4. Mix lemon juice with sugar and pour over the salad.
5. Add sugar, salt, pepper.

Nutritional Information:
Calories: 185
Total fat: 0.7 oz
Total carbohydrates: 0.5 oz
Protein: 0.3 oz

Mediterranean salad with spinach, dried tomatoes and feta cheese

Feel the spirit of the Mediterranean and ancient Greece with a salad of tomatoes dried on a bright amber sun, feta cheese and black olives. Feta cheese will add more calories to the salad and make it taste unforgettable.

Completion: 15 min
Prep time: 10 min
Serving: 2
Ingredients:
5 oz spinach
3 oz lettuce
7 oz sundried tomatoes
6 oz feta cheese

4 oz black olives
1 tomato
1 onion
4 tablespoons pumpkin seed oil
1 tablespoon soy sauce
1 tablespoon white wine vinegar
black ground pepper
chopped fresh parsley

How to Prepare:
1. Chop dried tomatoes, spinach, lettuce and onion.
2. Cut tomato.
3. Cut feta cheese into cubes.
4. Mix feta cheese with vegetables.
5. Add olives, salt, pepper, chopped fresh parsley.
6. Pour pumpkin seed oil, soy sauce, and white wine vinegar over salad.

Nutritional Information:
Calories: 401
Total fat: 2.7 oz
Total carbohydrates: 2.5 oz
Protein: 2 oz

Salad with avocado, cucumber and sesame seeds

Exotic taste! Green, light salad is easy to make and is packed with cucumber freshness.

Completion: 15 min
Prep time: 5 min
Serving: 2

Ingredients:
1 avocado
1 cucumber
4 oz spinach
1 oz broccoli
2 tablespoons canned peas

3 tablespoons soy sauce
1 tablespoon white wine vinegar
sea salt
black ground pepper
chopped fresh parsley

How to Prepare:

1. Peel avocado and cucumber.
2. Cut avocado into cubes and cucumber into half rings.
3. Boil broccoli for 10 minutes.
4. Chop spinach. Mix with avocado, broccoli, peas and cucumber.
5. Add salt, pepper.
6. Add chopped fresh parsley.
7. Pour soy sauce and white wine vinegar over salad.

Nutritional Information:
Calories: 165
Total fat: 0.7 oz
Total carbohydrates: 1.1 oz
Protein: 1 oz

Salad with carrots, radishes, raisins and walnuts

Light and fresh salad with carrots, radishes and walnuts is easy to make and packed with vitamins. Your vegan and vegetarian friends will love it!
Completion: 10 min
Prep time: 5 min
Serving: 2

Ingredients:

2 carrots
4 radishes
3 oz walnuts
4 oz raisins
2 tablespoons soy sauce
sea salt
black ground pepper
chopped fresh parsley

How to Prepare:

1. Peel the carrots.
2. Grate carrots and radishes in Korean style using a Korean carrot grater.
3. Mix carrots and radishes with walnuts and raisins.
4. Add salt, pepper.
5. Add chopped fresh parsley.
6. Pour soy sauce over salad.

Nutritional Information:

Calories: 155
Total fat: 0.9 oz
Total carbohydrates: 0.8 oz

Protein: 0.5 oz

Salad with cucumber, dried tomatoes and honey

Would you like to try something unforgettable? Then a salad with cucumber, dried tomatoes and honey is vegan salad you need to taste! This mix of different tastes will be a new experience.

Completion: 15 min
Prep time: 5 min
Serving: 2

Ingredients:

1 carrot
1 red bell pepper
1 cucumber
7 oz dried tomatoes
3 oz lettuce
4 oz raisins
5 tablespoons liquid honey
chopped fresh greenery

How to Prepare:

1. Peel and grate the carrot.
2. Cut bell pepper, cucumber and dried tomatoes into pieces.
3. Chop lettuce.
4. Mix vegetables with raisins.
5. Add chopped fresh greenery.
6. Pour honey over salad.

Nutritional Information:

Calories: 185
Total fat: 0.9 oz
Total carbohydrates: 0.8 oz
Protein: 0.7 oz

Salad with spinach and sesame seeds

Healthy spring, spinach salad with vitamins. Spinach contains a lot of iron in it, so it is vital diet element for children and adults. Sesame seeds are rich in vitamins and especially in calcium.

Completion: 15 min
Prep time: 5 min
Serving: 2

<u>Ingredients:</u>
7 oz fresh spinach
3 oz oats
3 oz cherry tomatoes
1 lemon
small bunch of chives
3 oz raisins
2 tablespoons sesame seeds

1 tablespoon honey
2 tablespoons sesame oil
sea salt
black pepper

How to Prepare:

1. Cut the spinach, tomatoes and chives into pieces.
2. Mix vegetables with oats and raisins.
3. Squeeze lemon juice, mix with honey and pour over salad.
4. Add sesame seeds and sesame oil.
5. Add salt and pepper.

Nutritional Information:

Calories: 203
Total fat: 2 oz
Total carbohydrates: 1.9 oz
Protein: 1.2 oz

Citrus salad with orange, grapefruit, kumquat and walnuts

Cheerful and colorful citrus salad will add freshness and positiveness to your life!

Completion: 20 min
Prep time: 10 min
Serving: 2

Ingredients:
1 orange
1 grapefruit
3 kumquats
3 oz walnuts
5 oz lettuce
1 oz feta cheese
1 tablespoon olive oil
1 teaspoon brown sugar
lime juice

How to Prepare:
1. Peel the orange.
2. Peel the grapefruit.
3. Cut orange, grapefruit and kumquats into segments.
4. Cut feta cheese into cubes.
5. Mix fruits with feta.
6. Add walnuts.
7. Mix olive oil, lime juice and sugar.
8. Pour olive oil and lime juice.

Nutritional Information:

Calories: 398
Total fat: 2 oz
Total carbohydrates: 1.5 oz
Protein: 1 oz

Exotic fruits light and sunny salad

Sunny and colorful exotic fruits salad could be made from any fruits you will find in your kitchen. To prepare such a dessert is very simple – just use any fruits that your family and children don't want to eat! Collect everything and make this incredible salad or use our ingredient suggestions below.

Completion: 10 min
Prep time: 10 min
Serving: 2
Ingredients:
1 pear
1 apple
2 kiwis
1 grapefruit
1 orange
1 banana
4 big strawberries

2 tablespoons sugar
1 cup cream
pineapple juice
dark chocolate
cinnamon

How to Prepare:

1. Mix cream and sugar using a mixer.
2. Peel and cut all the fruits into pieces.
3. Add fruits into bowls or glasses.
4. Pour pineapple juice over each serving.
5. Add mixed cream on top to each one.
6. Grate dark chocolate on top of the cream.
7. Add cinnamon. Bon Appetite!

Nutritional Information:

Calories: 358
Total fat: 2 oz
Total carbohydrates: 1.8 oz
Protein: 1.5 oz

Chapter III: Pasta

Pasta is a traditional and very old Italian dish. Nowadays it is popular in every world corner. It is simple and fast to prepare and cook, but the main advantage of pasta is that it has many variations. Pasta has no hard rules and you could create original recipes every day. Often you don't need special products, but just can use the one you have in your kitchen and fridge! What's more, if you don't have pasta, you could always use macaroni or even noodles instead.

Pasta with broccoli, green peas, beans and corn

If you are hungry then this delicious pasta recipe with lots of calories, carbohydrates and proteins will help you regain your strengths and vitality.
Completion: 50 min
Prep time: 10 min
Cooking time: 30 min
Serving: 4

Ingredients:
any type of pasta (15-17 oz)
5 oz fresh broccoli
1 can of canned beans
1 can of canned green peas
1 can of canned corn
2 crushed cloves of garlic
1 onion
2 carrots
1 tomato
sunflower oil

2 tablespoons of flour
2 tablespoons pumpkin seeds oil
4 tablespoons tomato paste
1 cup water
salt
red ground pepper
1 bunch fresh chopped parsley

How to Cook:

1. Boil the water and cook the pasta (follow the cooking time suggested on the packet). Add 1 tablespoon oil. In parallel, boil the carrots to half-cooked.
2. Chop onion.
3. Heat the oil and fry the onion for 2 min.
4. In the same oil, fry garlic for 1 min on a medium heat.
5. Add the tomato paste and mix with water.
6. Add flour and stir well.
7. Boil the sauce stirring over medium heat for 15 minutes.
8. Add canned beans, green peas and corns to the sauce and continue cooking for 12 minutes.
9. Add half of the chopped parsley to the sauce.
10. Cut boiled carrots into pieces.
11. Add carrots to the sauce.
12. Add salt and red pepper.
13. Close the lid and leave for 5-10 minutes, so that the sauce absorbs the flour.
14. Put the pasta into a bowl and top with sauce.
15. Cut tomatoes into pieces and put them on a plate with pasta.
16. Add parsley and pour pumpkin seed oil.

Nutritional Information:

Calories: 500
Total fat: 4.2 oz

Total carbohydrates: 4 oz
Protein: 3 oz

Pasta with champignons and cauliflower

Pasta with champignons and cauliflower is one of simplest recipes. It is not difficult to cook at all, but it is also very tasty. A simple set of ingredients makes it available for frequent use. Champignons and delicious creamy sauce with the aroma of Herbes de Provence will make the usual dinner a holiday for your friends and family.

Completion: 40 min
Prep time: 10 min
Cooking time: 30 min
Serving: 4

Ingredients:
any type of pasta (around 15-17 oz)
15 oz freshly chopped champignons (mushrooms)
5 oz cauliflower

2 onions
1 chopped garlic clove
2 tablespoons of flour
1 cup milk or cream
sunflower oil
2 oz parmesan cheese
half cup red wine
sea salt
black ground pepper
Herbes de Provence
1 bunch fresh chopped parsley

How to Cook:

1. Boil the water and cook the pasta (follow the cooking time suggested on the packet). Add 1 tablespoon oil. In parallel, boil the cauliflower to half-cooked.
2. When pasta is ready add 2 tablespoons olive oil. Later we will use water from the boiled pasta.
3. Let's get to the sauce now - chop champignons and onions.
4. Heat the oil and fry onions.
5. Add chopped garlic.
6. Add champignons and flour, cook for 20 min.
7. Pour water from boiled pasta and red wine and cook for 2 min.
8. Pour milk or cream and cook for 5 min.
9. Add boiled and chopped cauliflower to the sauce, and cook for 5 min with closed lid.
10. Add Herbes de Provence, some salt and pepper.
11. Grate parmesan cheese, and then add to the sauce.
12. Put pasta into the sauce and stir well.
13. Add parsley on top.

Nutritional Information:

Calories: 498
Total fat: 4.2 oz

Total carbohydrates: 4 oz
Protein: 3 oz

Pasta with tomato, bell pepper and spinach

Pasta with tomato, bell pepper and spinach is a perfect dish for those who value their time. It is very simple to cook, but gives a great dining experience for the whole family. Why is pasta the perfect product? The main reason is that pasta can be stored for a long time without a fridge. It is a staple of any home kitchen. The same goes for frozen spinach which can be kept safely in a fridge for a long period of time.

Completion: 30 min
Prep time: 10 min
Cooking time: 20 min
Serving: 3

Ingredients:
any type of pasta (10 oz)
4 oz cherry tomatoes
2 sweet fresh bell peppers
10 oz frozen spinach
2 onions
1 cup milk or cream
2 oz parmesan cheese
olive oil
ground sesame seeds
sea salt
black ground pepper
Herbes de Provence
1 bunch fresh chopped parsley
basil

How to Cook:
1. Boil the water and cook the pasta (follow the cooking time suggested on the packet). Add 1 tablespoon oil.

2. Add 2 tablespoons olive oil when pasta is ready. Later we will use water from the boiled pasta.
3. Let's get to the sauce now - chop fresh bell peppers and onions.
4. Put frozen spinach into a colander with hot water for 2 min.
5. After you remove the water mash spinach with the spoon.
6. Heat the oil and fry onions.
7. Add chopped, fresh bell peppers.
8. Add spinach.
9. Pour water from boiled pasta and cook for 10 min.
10. Pour milk or cream and cook for 5 min.
11. Add Herbes de Provence, salt, pepper, ground sesame seeds
12. Put pasta into the sauce and stir well.
13. Grate parmesan cheese, and then add to the sauce.
14. Cut cherry tomatoes into pieces and put them on a plate with pasta.
15. Add parsley and basil on top to garnish.

Nutritional Information:
Calories: 485
Total fat: 4 oz
Total carbohydrates: 3.5 oz
Protein: 3 oz

Pasta with eggplant and champignons

Pasta with eggplant and champignons is a perfect dish for the whole family. It is extremely delicious and fast to cook!

Completion: 30 min
Prep time: 15 min
Cooking time: 15 min
Serving: 3

Ingredients:
any type of pasta (10 oz)
1 eggplant
5 oz freshly chopped champignons (mushrooms)
1 onion
3 crushed cloves of garlic
4 tablespoons marinara sauce
2 tablespoons olive oil
cup of water
sea salt
black ground pepper
Herbes de Provence
1 bunch fresh chopped parsley

How to Cook:
1. Boil the water and cook the pasta (follow the cooking time suggested on the packet). Add 1 tablespoon oil
2. Add 2 tablespoons olive oil when pasta is ready. Later we will use water from the boiled pasta.
3. Let's get to the sauce now – cut the eggplant into cubes.
4. Chop champignons, garlic and onions.
5. Put the eggplant into a colander and sprinkle with salt. Leave it for 15 min.
6. Heat the oil and fry onions.
7. Add eggplant, garlic, champignons and fry until golden brown.
8. Pour a bit of water from boiled pasta and stew for 5 min
9. Set aside and cover for 5 min.
10. Add Herbes de Provence, some salt and pepper.
11. Put pasta into the sauce and stir well.
12. Add parsley on top.

Nutritional Information:
Calories: 475
Total fat: 2.1 oz

Total carbohydrates: 2 oz
Protein: 1 oz

Pasta with avocado, green peas and asparagus

A lot of Americans still associate pasta with the dine-in restaurant experience, but why not make it an everyday dish in the home kitchen? After all, mostly pasta recipes are not expensive, easy to cook and can make a worthy alternative to every day meals. Try this delicious pasta with avocado, green peas and asparagus!

Completion: 30 min
Prep time: 15 min
Cooking time: 15 min
Serving: 3

Ingredients:
any type of pasta (10 oz)
1 avocado
2 garlic cloves
4 asparagus
4 oz frozen green peas
2 tablespoons lemon juice
2 tablespoons water
sea salt
olive oil
black ground pepper
Herbes de Provence
basil

How to Cook:
1. Boil the water and cook the pasta (follow the cooking time suggested on the packet). Add 1 tablespoon oil.
2. 2 min before the pasta is ready add asparagus and green peas.
3. Add 2 tablespoons olive oil when pasta is ready.

4. Let's get to the sauce now – cut avocado into pieces.
5. Mix avocado and garlic using a blender.
6. Add water and lemon juice.
7. Mix pasta with avocado sauce and stir well.
8. Add asparagus and green peas.
9. Add Herbes de Provence, sea salt, pepper, basil.

Nutritional Information:

Calories: 445
Total fat: 2.2 oz
Total carbohydrates: 2 oz
Protein: 1 oz

Pasta with tomatoes, parmesan, gorgonzola cheese and lemon juice

This pasta recipe is very simple to cook, however, it still has a lot of calories because you use two famous Italian kinds of cheese with it - parmesan cheese and gorgonzola cheese.

Completion: 25 min
Prep time: 10 min
Cooking time: 15 min
Serving: 3

<u>Ingredients:</u>
Short pasta (e.g. fusilli, macaroni, penne) or a selection of your choice
13 oz tomatoes
2 oz parmesan cheese
2 oz gorgonzola cheese

2 garlic cloves
sea salt
olive oil
lemon juice
black ground pepper
Herbes de Provence
basil

How to Cook:
1. Boil the water and cook the pasta (follow the cooking time suggested on the packet). Add 1 tablespoon oil.
2. Add 2 tablespoons olive oil when pasta is ready.
3. Let's get to the sauce now – chop garlic and tomatoes.
4. Heat the oil and fry garlic in frying pan for 1 min, then add tomatoes.
5. Grate parmesan cheese, and then add to the frying pan.
6. Add pasta, stir well. If the sauce is too thick, you should add some hot water.
7. Grate gorgonzola cheese and add to the sauce.
8. Pour some lemon juice.
9. Add Herbes de Provence, sea salt, pepper.

Nutritional Information:
Calories: 650
Total fat: 3.5 oz
Total carbohydrates: 3 oz
Protein: 2 oz

Pasta with pumpkin sauce and orange juice

Pumpkin and orange juice creates an unforgettable taste. This pasta dish could be served not only for your family as an everyday meal, but also on special occasions. Enjoy!

Completion: 30 min
Prep time: 15 min
Cooking time: 15 min
Serving: 3
<u>**Ingredients:**</u>
any type of pasta
20 oz fresh tomatoes
20 oz pumpkin
1 onion
2 garlic cloves
1 cup orange juice
sunflower oil

sea salt
black ground pepper

How to Cook:
1. Boil the water and cook the pasta (follow the cooking time suggested on the packet). Add 1 tablespoon oil.
2. Add 2 tablespoons olive oil when pasta is ready.
3. Let's get to the sauce now – chop garlic and onions.
4. Peel the pumpkin and cube it.
5. Heat the oil and fry garlic and onions for 1 min.
6. Add pumpkin and fry for 5 min.
7. Pour orange juice and stir well.
8. Close the lid for 5 min.
9. Cut tomatoes and add them to a frying pan, cook for 5 min.
10. Add pasta, stir well.
11. Grate gorgonzola cheese and add to the sauce.
12. Add sea salt and pepper to serve.

Nutritional Information:
Calories: 345
Total fat: 2.8 oz
Total carbohydrates: 2.5 oz
Protein: 2 oz

Delicious and romantic pasta for 2 with vegetable mix

This pasta recipe could be used as a romantic dinner served with a wine. But also you can double the ingredients and then it could be served to a larger group of friends or family. It is simple and fast to cook due to its basic ingredients.

Completion: 30 min
Prep time: 15 min
Cooking time: 15 min
Serving: 2

<u>Ingredients:</u>
any type of pasta (e.g. macaroni or noodles)
2 carrots
2 onions

1 broccoli
stem of fresh celery
olive oil
sea salt
black ground pepper
red ground pepper
Herbes de Provence
basil

How to Cook:
1. Boil the water and cook the pasta (follow the cooking time suggested on the packet). Add 1 tablespoon of oil.
2. Add 2 tablespoons olive oil when pasta is ready. Later we will use water from the boiled pasta.
3. Let's get to the sauce now – peel and cut carrots into rings.
4. Cut onions into rings.
5. Cut the broccoli into pieces.
6. Cut celery into pieces.
7. Heat the oil and fry onions for 1 min until golden brown.
8. Add chopped carrots, broccoli and celery, stew for 10 min with closed lid.
9. Pour water from boiled pasta and cook for 5 min.
10. Put vegetables (sauce) into the pasta and stir.
11. Add Herbes de Provence, salt, black and red pepper.
12. Put pasta into plates.
13. Add basil on top to serve.

Nutritional Information:
Calories: 335
Total fat: 2.8 oz
Total carbohydrates: 2.7 oz
Protein: 2 oz

Chapter IV: Raw Food Recipes

Raw food is very healthy, because we eat vegetables and fruits with all the vitamins provided by nature. We don't boil, don't cook, and don't fry, because during those processes our food loses a lot of vital elements.

Vegetarian burger with cucumber, avocado and champignon

Burgers do not always need to contain a fatty piece of meat. Try the recipe of this vegetarian burger with cucumber, avocado and champignon. This is a great idea for those who want to experience a burger with a difference.

Completion: 15 min
Prep time: 10 min
Cooking time: 5 min
Serving: 1

Ingredients:
1 burger bun
1 cucumber
1 avocado
1 champignon
1 red onion
lime juice or orange juice
pumpkin seed oil
sea salt
black ground pepper
red ground pepper

How to Prepare:
1. Cut cucumber into rounds.
2. Cut red onion into rings.

3. Cut champignon into pieces.
4. Peel and cut half of the avocado into pieces.
5. Smash the other half of the avocado with fork or spoon.
6. Add lime juice or orange juice, pumpkin seed oil and sea salt, stir well and paste is ready.
7. Cut burger bun in half.
8. Put burger bun into a toaster or fry for 1 min on a frying pan.
9. Put paste on a burger bun.
10. Add red onion rings, cucumber rings, champignon rings on top.
11. Add sea salt, black ground pepper, red ground pepper.
12. Add avocado and pour with pumpkin seed oil.
13. Add second half of burger bun on top!

Nutritional Information:

Calories: 226
Total fat: 1.4 oz
Total carbohydrates: 1.2 oz
Protein: 1 oz

Vegetarian farm burger with potatoes, tomatoes, onions and corn

Actually, this type of burger you can make from the ingredients you have in your kitchen! Somewhere deep in your fridge, you will always find some veggies, few tomatoes or canned corn! This is a great idea for those who want prepare healthy and quick dish from ingredients they have at home.

Completion: 15 min
Prep time: 10 min
Cooking time: 5 min
Serving: 1

Ingredients:
1 burger bun
1 mid-size potato

1 tomato
2 radishes
1 small cucumber
2 onions
lettuce
canned corns
sunflower oil
butter
sea salt
black ground pepper
red ground pepper
dried dill

How to Prepare:

1. Cut tomato, radishes and cucumber into rings.
2. Cut onion into rings.
3. Boil potato and onion.
4. Smash potato and onion with fork or spoon in a bowl.
5. Add butter, sunflower oil or pumpkin seed oil, sea salt and red pepper, dried dill, stir well.
6. Heat the oil and fry half of the onion for 1-2 min until golden brown.
7. Cut burger bun in half.
8. Put burger bun into a toaster or fry for 1 min on a frying pan.
9. Put paste on a burger bun.
10. Add fried onion on top.
11. Add tomato, onion, radish, cucumber rings, some canned corns and lettuce on top.
12. Add sea salt, black ground pepper, red ground pepper.
13. Add second half of burger bun on top!

Nutritional Information:
Calories: 236
Total fat: 1.5 oz

Total carbohydrates: 1.3 oz
Protein: 1 oz

Delicious zucchini, walnuts, corn and sweet bell peppers rolls

You will fall in love with these delicious zucchini, walnuts, corn and sweet bell peppers rolls from the first fork. The fresh, young zucchini and sweet corns with peppers will melt in your mouth. You can serve it to your best friends at your home when all the dishes are old and common.

Completion: 20 min
Prep time: 10 min
Cooking time: 10 min
Serving: 2

Ingredients:
1 young fresh zucchini
cup of walnuts
1 sweet bell pepper
2 carrots
2 garlic cloves
1 can of canned corn
lime juice
sea salt
black ground pepper
red ground pepper
soy sauce
oregano

How to Prepare:
1. Put walnuts into the water to soak for about an hour.
2. Mash soaked walnuts using a blender.
3. Add garlic and mix together in a blender.
4. Cut sweet bell peppers, carrots into small pieces.
5. Mix all the vegetables using a blender.

6. Pour lime juice. Blend.
7. Add sea salt, black ground pepper, red ground pepper, oregano and canned corn. Blend.
8. Cut zucchini into longitudinal strips.
9. Wrap the vegetables into zucchini strips.
10. Stick a toothpick into them.
11. Pour soy sauce on top to serve.

Nutritional Information:
Calories: 189
Total fat: 1.5 oz
Total carbohydrates: 1 oz
Protein: 0.8 oz

Raw Gazpacho with grapes, strawberries and dried tomatoes

This delicious gazpacho with grapes, strawberries and dried tomatoes subtly remind us about hot and sunny summer days! It has a delicate texture, creamy taste and a truly summery aroma of strawberries. What's more, to prepare it you need only 20 minutes.

Completion: 20 min
Prep time: 10 min
Cooking time: 10 min
Serving: 3

Ingredients:

3 large sweet tomatoes
1 small sweet red pepper
7 berries of strawberry
2 oz grapes without seeds
1 medium cucumber (without skin)
1 cup dried tomatoes
1 red onion
2 cloves of garlic
orange juice
red ground pepper
chili pepper (chili)
sea salt
basil

How to Prepare:
1. Wash vegetables.
2. Cut tomatoes, sweet red pepper, cucumber, red onion, garlic into pieces.
3. Then smash all the vegetables, strawberries, grapes, dried tomatoes using a blender until the mixture becomes a homogeneous cream soup.
4. Pour orange juice.
5. Add sea salt, red ground pepper, chili pepper.
6. Pour gazpacho on plates or into glasses, decorating with a leaf of basil.

Nutritional Information:
Calories: 156
Total fat: 1.7 oz
Total carbohydrates: 1 oz
Protein: 0.7 oz

Spaghetti from a zucchini with mango and blueberry sauce

A bright, sunny treat for long-awaited friends and family. No need to stew, boil or fry!

Completion: 20 min
Prep time: 10 min
Cooking time: 10 min
Serving: 2

Ingredients:
1 young zucchini
1.5 oz hazelnuts
2 oz blueberries
half cup unflavored yogurt
1 mango
2 cloves of garlic
orange juice
pumpkin seed oil
sea salt
basil

How to Prepare:
1. Grate zucchini in Korean style using a Korean carrot grater.
2. Let's get to the sauce now – cut up mango and garlic.
3. Add orange juice into a blender.
4. Smash hazelnuts, blueberries, yogurt, mango, garlic using a blender.
5. Mix the sauce with zucchini spaghetti.
6. Add pumpkin seed oil on top.
7. Add basil on top!

Nutritional Information:

Calories: 149
Total fat: 1.7 oz
Total carbohydrates: 1.2 oz
Protein: 1 oz

Chapter V: Desserts

Sweet and healthy? Could it be in the same dish? Yes, it could! Try our veg light desserts! Use them as a base to invent your own recipes, experiment, play, enjoy!

Cherry smoothie with almond milk

This sunny cherry smoothie with almond milk is ideal for bright, hot summer days! It is fast to make and full of vitamins.

Completion: 10 min
Prep time: 10 min
Serving: 2

Ingredients:

10 oz of cherries (frozen or fresh)
1 oz blueberries (frozen or fresh)
1 oz strawberries (frozen or fresh)
1 banana
2 oz almonds
1 cup orange juice
2 teaspoons of honey
1 cup of almond milk
dark chocolate

How to Prepare:
1. Mix cherries, blueberries, strawberries, banana, almonds using a blender.
2. Add orange juice, honey.
3. Pour almond milk.
4. Mix well using a mixer.
5. Grate dark chocolate on top - and your smoothie is ready!

Nutritional Information:
Calories: 129
Total fat: 2 oz
Total carbohydrates: 1.5 oz
Protein: 1.2 oz

Rice pudding with coconut milk

Rice pudding with coconut milk is delicious and tasty dessert for romantic dinner.

Completion: 35 min
Prep time: 10 min
Cooking time: 25 min
Serving: 2

Ingredients:

1 can of coconut milk
1 cup round-grained white rice
half cup of maple syrup
1 tablespoon vanilla
1 tablespoon ground cinnamon
1 cup almond milk
2 tablespoons brown sugar
1 cup of raisins

How to Prepare:
1. Pour coconut milk into a saucepan and boil.
2. Rinse and dry the rice, then add it to the milk.
3. Stir occasionally for 5 min., reduce heat, cover with the lid and stew for 20 min.
4. Add maple syrup, vanilla, cinnamon, almond milk, brown sugar and mix well.
5. At this stage, you can add washed raisins.
6. Cook for another 10 minutes. Rice should absorb a lot of liquid.
7. Stir often so that rice does not stick to the bottom of the pan.

8. Remove the pudding from the heat and let it cool for at least 5 minutes.

9. Pudding is ready! Now you can serve it both warm and cold.

Nutritional Information:

Calories: 125
Total fat: 2 oz
Total carbohydrates: 1.5 oz
Protein: 1 oz

Chocolate mousse with mango and almonds

Chocolate has a lot of calories in it. Moreover, dark and milk chocolate contains a lot of vital vitamins that are crucial for our body and health, such as magnesium, iron, vitamin B12 and many others. So this mousse is not only very tasty, but also together with mango and almonds, it is very healthy!

Completion: 30 min
Prep time: 10 min
Cooking time: 20 min
Serving: 2

Ingredients:
1 mango
10 oz dark chocolate
5 oz milk chocolate
1 cup cream

2 tablespoons brown sugar
1 teaspoon vanilla
2 oz almonds

How to Prepare:

1. Cut mango into strips.
2. Melt dark and milk chocolate. Allow chocolate to cool down.
3. Smash almonds using a blender.
4. Whisk cream with a mixer until the foam and add sugar.
5. Add vanilla and almonds.
6. Gradually, whisking, bring the cooled chocolate mass into the cream.
7. Put the chocolate mousse in the crockery, small bowls or cups.
8. Add mango strips on top.
9. Add few almonds.
10. Grate some chocolate on top.
11. Before serving, put the chocolate mousse into the refrigerator for an hour. Bon Appetite!

Nutritional Information:

Calories: 490
Total fat: 3.9 oz
Total carbohydrates: 2.7 oz
Protein: 2.5 oz

Light pumpkin, coconut and orange mousse

Pumpkin is a real miracle. It is a vegetable full of minerals and vitamins, such as B1, B6, PP, K and others that are responsible for the different key processes in our body. It contains a lot of carotenes - vitamin A - that is four and a half times higher in pumpkin than in carrots. Pumpkin is also very tasty! If you prepare the mousse from the pumpkin adding coconut and lemon you will feel the airiness and tenderness in your mouth while tasting it and this dish will become your favorite dessert.

Completion: 30 min
Prep time: 10 min
Cooking time: 20 min
Serving: 2

Ingredients:
12 oz pumpkin

4 oz coconut flakes
half cup coconut milk
5 oz semolina
5 tablespoons brown sugar
1 teaspoon vanilla
half cup orange juice

How to Prepare:
1. Peel the pumpkin.
2. Cut pumpkin into pieces and boil for 15 min.
3. Boil semolina with sugar and coconut milk for 5 min. You need to stir all the time.
4. Cool down semolina and mix with pumpkin and water where it was boiled.
5. Add orange juice, vanilla and coconut flakes.
6. Mix everything using a mixer for 10 min.
7. Before serving, put the mousse into the refrigerator for an hour. Bon Appetite!

Nutritional Information:
Calories: 480
Total fat: 3.7 oz
Total carbohydrates: 2.5 oz
Protein: 2.4 oz

Kiwi and yogurt with walnuts and honey

This is perfect for a light breakfast. Cooking this dish is very simple and fast. Pump your body with the energy for the day ahead!

Completion: 10 min
Prep time: 10 min
Serving: 2

Ingredients:
2 kiwis
1.5 oz walnuts
1 cup yogurt or cream
2 tablespoons sugar
2 tablespoons oat brans
2 tablespoons liquid honey
2 tablespoons blueberries

dark chocolate

How to Prepare:
1. Peel and dice kiwis.
2. Put the first level of kiwis into the bowl.
3. Add walnuts.
4. Add oat brans.
5. Add sugar
6. Pour liquid honey.
7. Pour yogurt or cream on top.
8. Add the second slice of kiwis and put all ingredients on top as previous.
9. Add blueberries.
10. Grate dark chocolate on top to serve.

Nutritional Information:
Calories: 187
Total fat: 1.7 oz
Total carbohydrates: 1 oz
Protein: 0.9 oz

Blueberry cocktail with yogurt and honey

Blueberries are traditional North America berries. These indigo-colored berries have lots of vitamins. One of the best ways to eat blueberries is raw or to serve with milk products. Our blueberry cocktail with yogurt and honey will add some traditional cuisine tastes into your eating routine!

Completion: 20 min
Prep time: 10 min
Cooking time: 10 min
Serving: 3

<u>Ingredients:</u>

10 oz blueberry
2 cups yogurt
2 tablespoons liquid honey
strawberry syrup
half cup milk
2 oz cream ice cream
1 tablespoon brown sugar
vanilla
cinnamon

How to Prepare:
1. Mix blueberries, honey, yogurt, sugar, vanilla using a blender.
2. Pour into glasses.
3. Mix milk, strawberry syrup and ice cream using a blender.
4. Pour into glasses with the blueberries mixture.
5. Grate cinnamon and place on top to serve.

Nutritional Information:
Calories: 530
Total fat: 4.5 oz
Total carbohydrates: 4.2 oz
Protein: 3.9 oz

Yogurt with banana

Sweet-sour yogurt and banana breakfast. This dish is very simple, so it will take you around 5 to 10 min to prepare it.

Completion: 10 min
Prep time: 5 min
Serving: 1

Ingredients:
1 cup unflavored yogurt
1 banana
half cup of maple syrup
1 tablespoon vanilla
1 tablespoon ground cinnamon
2 tablespoons brown sugar

How to Prepare:
1. Cut the banana into rings.
2. Put the first level of banana into the bowl.
3. Add yogurt, sugar and vanilla.
4. Put the second level of banana into the bowl.
5. Add yogurt, sugar and vanilla.
6. Pour maple syrup.
7. Pour yogurt on top.

Nutritional Information:
Calories: 195
Total fat: 2 oz
Total carbohydrates: 2.3 oz
Protein: 2 oz

Kiwi and banana mousse

Light and refreshing kiwi and banana mousse could be served during hot summer days or on special occasions!
Completion: 20 min
Prep time: 10 min
Serving: 2

Ingredients:
4 kiwis
1 banana
2 avocados
1 orange
1 tablespoon ground cinnamon
2 tablespoons brown sugar
2 tablespoons liquid honey
few mint leaves
dark chocolate

How to Prepare:
1. Squeeze the orange juice.
2. Peel the fruits and mix them using a blender.
3. Add orange juice, honey, sugar, cinnamon, mint leaves and mix using a blender.
4. Before serving, put the mousse into the refrigerator for 1 hour.
5. Grate cinnamon and dark chocolate on top. Bon Appetite!

Nutritional Information:
Calories: 176
Total fat: 1.8 oz

Total carbohydrates: 1.9 oz
Protein: 1.5 oz

Strawberry mousse

Raw strawberry is a perfect dessert without any additional ingredients, sugars and others! Bright red color berries are perfect decoration at any table. Besides the unusual bright color and unforgettable aroma, this berry is very rich in vitamins and minerals. It is strongly recommended to eat strawberries daily, as it cleanses the blood. Of course, it is best to eat strawberries in fresh form, but if you want new tastes and diversity, prepare strawberry mousse. It's very simple to cook, tasty and beautiful. Such an easy, sweat, aromatic dessert will please both adults and children.

Completion: 25 min
Prep time: 10 min
Cooking time: 15 min
Serving: 4

Ingredients:
2 cups strawberries
7 tablespoons brown sugar
1 tablespoons liquid honey
5 tablespoons semolina
vanilla
dark chocolate
cinnamon

How to Prepare:
1. Mix strawberries, honey, and vanilla using a blender.
2. Boil semolina with sugar for 5 min. You need to stir all the time.
3. Add smashed strawberries, stir well and cool down.
4. Mix everything using a mixer for 10 min.
5. Before serving, put the mousse into the refrigerator for 2 hours.
6. Grate cinnamon and dark chocolate on top. Bon Appetite!

Nutritional Information:
Calories: 290
Total fat: 2.3 oz
Total carbohydrates: 1.9 oz
Protein: 1 oz

Conclusion

This book includes different vegetarian and vegan recipes, such as soups, salads, pasta, raw dishes, and desserts. You can find interesting, and sometimes unusual, recipes that will inspire you to cook tasty and delicious dishes. Often you should just use your imagination, because there is no limit what you can cook. This vegetarian and vegan book hasn't all the recipes. It was written to show you a direction and to inspire you to discover a rich and colorful world of vegetarian and vegan cooking!

If you are new in this field of vegetarian cuisine, this book will help you to start your cooking journey. The recipes in this book are simple, and the process of cooking and preparing dishes is explained in the simple way. We also added some more complex recipes. Those you can cook, when you level of experience will grow and you will feel more confident. But never give up, always be open to learn and try something new!

77623568R00051

Made in the USA
Middletown, DE
23 June 2018